THE GARLAND KING

Matthew Hedley Stoppard was born in Derbyshire in 1985. After a brief career as a journalist, he now works as a librarian, and lives in Otley with his wife and two sons.

Recordings of Matthew's poetry include *Insect Eucharist and Other Poems* (2012) and the spoken-word album *Runt County* (2014), both available from Adult Teeth Recordings. On the page, his poetry has appeared in *Magma, Iota, Cake, The Morning Star, A Complicated Way of Being Ignored* (Grist, 2012) and *Holding Your Hand Through Hard Times* (Osset Originals, 2014).

Matthew's debut collection of poetry, *A Family Behind Glass*, was published by Valley Press in 2013, and was included in the *Guardian*'s Readers' Books of the Year. His next publication was *Cinema Stories* (2015), a collaboration with fellow Leeds-based poet James Nash, celebrating the movie theatres of Leeds, past and present.

The Garland King

MATTHEW HEDLEY STOPPARD

Valley Press

First published in 2020 by Valley Press
Woodend, The Crescent, Scarborough, YO11 2PW
www.valleypressuk.com

ISBN 978-1-912436-51-4
Cat. no. VP0172

Cover design by Jamie McGarry.
Cover illustration by Ben Edge.
Text design by Peter Barnfather.
Edited by Martha Sprackland.

Printed and bound in Great Britain by
Imprint Digital, Upton Pyne, Exeter.

Contents

congregation of thugs 11

The Virgin Mary, from the junior-school nativity,
   after inhaling aerosols 12

We entered St Ecgwin's, Godless and poor,
   and saw a wren 14

Collecting post from a previous address 15

Well Dressing 16

Quite contrary 18

A mummer reflects on his child's tumour 20

Walking into a fist 21

Slot Song 22

May Day 23

Riding the stang 25

Most of the cargo was dead before the accident 26

One more carnivore 27

Balter 28

I embrace the Burryman 30

The Garland King 32

Shaman 33

Brace 37

Gallows Hill 38

Study of a Leeds bachelor 39

Bruises beneath feathers 40

Our urchin 42

Lawrence's voice 43

Killing a rat with an air rifle 44

Discovery on the outskirts of Matlock 45

Now he fears eggs 46

A man sees his own name on a park bench plaque 47

Eclipse plumage 49

Reveille   50
Three navigators, 1846   51
A haunting at Armley Library   53
Family pet used as costume for a folk play   54
A year's trigger   55
A busker leaves the brothel on York Road   57
Whitsuntide dray restored and paraded through
    Clay Cross, 2020   58
witch   60
Poem that features lines from a song heard in
    Stoney Middleton   61

Notes on the Text   63
Acknowledgements   65

The wake departed, and the guysers came. There was loud applause, and shouting and excitement as the old mystery play of St George, in which every man present had acted as a boy, proceeded, with banging and thumping of club and dripping pan.

– D.H. Lawrence, 'The Rainbow'

Now, when I'm dead and a-gone to my grave,
A decent funeral it's let me have,
So when I'm in my grave they may speak the truth:
"There lies a wild and wicked youth."

– traditional, 'Newry Town'

congregation of thugs

more and more we find ourselves   denim-clad
with arteries of crooked church lead cluttering the flat
and you can't move for bicycles without front wheels,
empty cans of Special Brew – all to be traded at the scrapyard

him over there tells anecdotes like an umbrella
opening up the arse   about his beginnings as a collection-plate thief
and lipsticking dirty limericks on dressing room mirrors
belonging to magicians' assistants at Batley Variety Club

don't believe any of it   we have to burglarise
truths here but I don't mind a good lie being broken into
sin shines on gold teeth when saying: "this is not
an electronic tag; it is an anklet for you, my love"

muscle is hard to come by but we have this wiry one
who can bore through any blockade –
I can count on him to sing: "if I had a hammer I'd cave
your head in"   and bring a shotgun to hook-a-duck

where do I fit in? I possess the plans   the visions
I can see your bones knit following a fracture sustained
falling from a drainpipe   these men listen when I stand
above them like a stained-glass saint to outline our next move

The Virgin Mary, from the junior-school nativity, after inhaling aerosols

Ours is a town that eats
egg and soldiers with shit still on the shell,
men tickle trout into submission
women mothers
                    of all –
days timed to a domino tap
when a player can't match spots,
the shortest member of the darts team
aiming for 19s rather than 20s.

"Mine is a bitch that squats
with her back to the wind
and catches
                    blackbirds midair
in her soft lips," boasts one uncle,
spaniel lapping from an ashtray
under a Miners Welfare table
stood on
wrought-iron
                    lion legs.

                    Piss-up of gnats
where my halo once hovered,
skin pure as foam
on a pint of Mansfield Bitter,
hidden in brambles and torn carrier bags,
                    a god in my belly,
its father graduated Sunday School,
was a crackshot with .22 rifle at air cadets,
can coil playground-swing chains round the frame
        in a one-er...

a ghost in my guts,
lungs filled with Glade,
camphor, capgun smoke...

I pucker for the nozzle
covering my head with a teatowel.

We entered St Ecgwin's,
Godless and poor, and saw a wren

tumbling from an organ pipe like a whimper
growing weaker at each attempt
      to entice her with whistles and broken wafers
she must have been trapped inside for weeks
stacked kneelers speckled with droppings
feathers floating on fontwater
    where she'd bathed
        or hoped to be reborn
we propped open the door with a parish newsletter
but she flew low towards the damp chancel walls
an eight-hundred-year-old ache in the stones for a saviour
      now our ache
a blemish in the air
    blurred overhead
        then perched on prayer numbers
she hid behind a wooden angel in the nave roof truss
we waited beneath until dark
    like an empty collection plate
until the curate's footsteps approached
and we fled across the cabbage field
      prison floodlights in the distance showing the way

Collecting post from a previous address

He beat his fists against the bus;
  to contain us passengers
the driver shushed shut the accordion doors.

From the upper deck I watched him
  snapping windscreen wipers
    and cracking cobwebs in the glass.

  In a tombola turn of nerves he roared
and ripped at the advertising poster
along the side, an encased audience

aghast at the rage-drunk dumpling man
throwing punches for every rumour
or whisper thrown over garden fences.

  Rattling metal panels from their screws,
embedding his fingers into taunts heard
throughout the years, tearing the vowels from "love" –

alone with the others, I watched him,
my heart, with the tremors of his efforts,
  thumped my ribs like a boxing-glove.

Well Dressing

For the one filled with Mum's donated blood,
how she'd come home frail as a dandelion clock,
blue tabard, cotton wool taped inside
her elbow, earrings like cablecars,
I built Eden (from an illustrated Bible she bought to stop me
feeling scared when the house was empty), ivy and cow parsley,
fag-ends for Eve's flesh, the snake a knitted draught-excluder.

For the one fermenting my step-dad's homebrew,
how he held me like a kitten
by the scruff of the neck, stumbling upstairs,
I used rabbit scuts for Moses' beard,
hops for his robes, and peeled beermats
scribbled in betting-shop pen
as his second set of commandment stones.

For the one containing an infection the surgeon drained
from my firstborn's pelvis (it neared
his lungs) the way he limped around
the kitchen the day he was admitted,
I built the story of David and Goliath entirely out of Lego
reclaimed from our Hoover bag – it's the least I could do
to atone for being such a clueless parent – sweetpeas to mask
the guilt and bags under my eyes and frame the scene.

For the one brimming with birthing-pool water, oily amniotic fluid
(and promises to do better as a father)
floating around my secondborn and his mother
I constructed the Nativity using conkers,
love-in-the-mist, and a biohazard bag emptied of placenta
for the donkey and manger, veil and halo.

This leaves nothing for the one holding Sunday League phlegm,
cold tea from a miner's snap tin, trickles from cracks in
    Whaley Bridge dam,
watered-down whisky none of us noticed at breakfast –
a county so stoic that if you flicked a shilling
into its history to make a wish
you wouldn't hear a splash.

Quite contrary

Fat worms shining in a wet dawn writhed into the back garden of No.19 Kenning Street. So effortlessly they plunged beneath the loose earth to swaddle themselves in soil.

Onion stalks collapsed under the weight of snails while sprawling squashes and marrows bordered the rest of the vegetables.

The woman from the house unlatched the three-inch-thick gate, following the path to the doorless privy, which housed everything she dug up the previous day. A ritual for the newlyweds at No.17 was to watch her put together a selection of produce in a crate, place a dahlia, plucked from her serried flowerbed, on top, and then leave it on the back wall.

For years all types from the town would take something on their way to work. Her onions were so sweet the factory workers would eat them raw, chomping on them like apples, during their teabreaks. The dahlias she grew were so bold and heavy-petalled that those who pinned them on their lapels looked like rosette-wearing councillors. She didn't ask for money and didn't expect it, but it was understood to leave her and the garden alone – even the tomcats knew not to spray there.

It was on a night when air was close that the husband was woken by the heat. Getting out of bed and opening the window, he heard nextdoor moving about in her kitchen. She appeared in the garden with a pram, wheeling her way to the marrows, tucking two of them into it. Then he watched her step into the greenhouse where she sang hymns to the tomatoes in a ragdoll-soft voice.

The husband thought he should turn away when she untied her dressing gown and hitched up her nightie to her collarbone, but he gazed on as she lowered herself to the vegetable patch, pressing her bare breasts into a freshly dug trench lined with onion bulbs. She stood up brushing soil and fat worms off her torso and thighs. And just before returning to bed, she pushed a nipple into the head of a dahlia, as if nourishing its stamen.

A mummer reflects on his child's tumour

In comes I, Bold Slasher   a lisp hinders
your way of saying "surrender"
aiming the bow and arrow (a sucker on the end)
ribbons and armour before we've had breakfast
      early morning appointments, nerves making me
want to retch, watching CBeebies in the oncology ward

I yield kneeling to feel for the lump
pains within and pains without
that has burnt a hole in your skull   killed more
than any battle   such a patronising prick, welling-up
because the really ill kid shared his paints with us
in the crafting area
    falling backwards
the arrow ricochets off my chest

a fist shoved in my mouth doesn't stifle the sobs
    you don't believe me when I say I'm doing a poo
you lower the weapon   *is there a doctor to be found*
skip into another room and return wearing
a toy stethoscope   I was a nob to the one who made you squeal
trying to take off your T-shirt, tiny torso on the X-ray table
    she was only trying to help, dickhead
remove my heart
breathe on it until it glows   *to heal this ghastly wound*
bringing me back to life   your brother enters
In comes I, Beelzebub   trying to hit me with a club
I love you equally, I hope that shows

Walking into a fist

According to reports, I deserved it.
Spilling out the arse-end of a house party,
spouting outrageous claims about someone's mother;
he thumped the stale beer out of my guts
then the sixth-form smile off my face.
I thought they were reserved for cartoon coyotes
concussed by falling anvils, but those stars
orbited my head after his heavy right-hook.
It felt like my jaw had met a ship's anchor
staggering back into a ringside of conifers.
Laying there, covered in giddiness and blood,
the garden gnomes giggled on picnic blankets –
teatowels blown from the washing line above –
and my outlook was a taxi headlights constellation.
Keeping that in mind, though I'd argue that I'm a bit brighter
I still struggle to dim
my temper.

Slot Song

Gladiators pummelled their opponents
with giant cotton buds when the timer below the screen flashed:
3.00, 2.59, 2.58...
Uncrossing my legs, I stood to raid our 'pound pot'
and dropped a coin in the Radio Rentals box –
not long before the gas meter cried out for cash
underneath the stairs.

Fibreglass biplanes and Postman Pat's van
were coin-operated, too; a twist and clunk
secured my leisure-centre locker,
released a ball of bubblegum.
50p lit a mile of baize in the snooker hall,
and paid the ransom for a Snickers held hostage
in a vending machine.

We'd cough up for jukebox and pinball;
emptied our pockets to NUDGE pineapples in a line.
The endless change we'd feed a condom dispenser,
inflating them on our heads until we were cartoon spacemen
reeking of Lynx and spermicide...

After all of this, I am starting to question
the custom of placing coins on a corpse's eyelids.

May Day

Meet us where the whippet lifts his leg
under the dead spider suspended in its web

we were up long before the day-o

Yes, I decorated my bonnet with plastic flowers from the cemetery
Yes, I goaded the ewe with the muck-caked arse
and chucked grit at crows bossing the waterlogged field
Yes, I startled an angler holding a perch
like he holds his manhood
                    sorry, love, I failed to teach the boys to piss
standing up and they stained the skirting board again

to welcome in the summer
to welcome in the May-o

Dogshit-bags garland a birch
when we gather on the hill
skipping, plaiting ribbons, smacking hazel branches, singing
                    did I tell you that I followed the kids round the house
last night, turning the lights off when they left the room?

Hal-an-Tow, Hal-an-Tow
jolly rumble-o

Dawn comes gaudy as pheasant feathers
sweat sticks smocks to the skin
                    it's time to play your favourite game show:
when did I last have a shower?
Our crowns of ivy and oxeye daisies wither and crisp
we are the first to be cremated

long before the day-o

Neither the fillings in our teeth nor the bells on our shins remain
and up goes the town and its bungalowed cul-de-sacs
        I torture myself for not putting a strawberry punnet
in the green bin, for not pulling the right face in the playground
and the melodeon wheezes its last
from the virus in its bellows

Riding the stang

Here we come with a ran, dan, dang;
It's not for you, nor for me, we ride this stang
But for Gooseberry Bob, whose wife he did bang.

Ladles pound saucepans
like Mum being throttled against the wall
between your bedroom and hers.

To keep the rabble at bay,
you tear out those rain-wrinkled images
first found behind Kwik Save:
arthritic pang of a reader's wife reclining,
stockings sagging, same bobbed hair as your nan.
You tear out the guts of those VHS tapes
from your teens
and hang them from a streetlamp,
hoping this makeshift Maypole of black ribbon
distracts the mob approaching.
Now you're Gooseberry Bob;
never raised a fist, like he did,
but there are girls
locked in your screen.

Ale to dilute tears,
sinking pints and pool balls –
one day you'll be manly enough
to wear overalls…

Here they come,
rolling pins beating baking trays,
animal clamour,
the letterbox rattling
like a bad case of nerves.

Most of the cargo was dead before the accident

Not an ambulance in sight,
the bodies bringing rush hour to a halt.
Fin on chevron, gills inhaling petrol fumes
gurnard staring into cats' eyes;
all of which called to my inner junior reporter,
shorthand crawling towards my fingers.
Refrain from puns such as "GUTTED!"
or "LARGE-SCALE TAILBACKS". Whiplashed
cod, coley, haddock and sprats delayed
a quarter of East Yorkshire's workforce,
iced salmon hogging the fast lane.
Police cordoned off the spilled polystyrene
boxes surrounding the jack-knifed lorry,
lobsters twitching inside, net-bags of mussels
clamping and unclamping on the central reservation –
there was no mention of "crash"
or "15 tonnes of wasted fresh fish"
in that day's horoscope for Pisces.
And it never occurred to the authorities
to dredge the motorway to clear up the scene,
an unsuccessful Feeding of Five Thousand to stop
the approaching rapture of seagulls.

One more carnivore

after Wim Delvoye

Slaughtermen smirked opening the sty gate,
the pink stampede saved from an electric current
or steel bolt through the brain and severed jugular vein.
Jewish and Islamic ovens were never a concern for them
but now they fear the canvas of a Belgian
wearing tortoise shell spectacles and a cigarette snarl
as he tattoos sailors, catfish and mutilated
Disney characters onto the hides of sedated swine.

Dogs chewing dried ears is a diorama enough
for anyone without the act being inked in as a concept.
Has the needling artist thought of recording
the symphony of squeals when the curly tail is yanked,
the percussive oinks during truffle snuffling?
We'll remember the marbling in streaky bacon –
a cheap cut preserving poverty and flavour – as we sit
down to dinner to gnaw on sculpture,
use abstract paintings as napkins – we will decide
if our art can be unlocked with a Spam-tin key.

Balter

"Although Morris dances are performed regularly in various parts of the country, their existence is bound to be tenuous whilst they rely upon the memory and ability of the men that perform them"
— Herbert C. MacIlwaine and Cecil J. Sharp, 'The Morris Book (Parts 1, 2 & 3)'

couldn't get a Rizla between his feet and the floor?
well, you couldn't get a man-sized tissue between me and a breakdown before this
feel here, scrimshaw across my skull each time I buckle
these bells to my shins   the older ones are slow and lovehandled
but I'd rather they taught me to caper than buy a pair of New Balance
and start jogging when the doctor says exercise helps with anxiety

escaped bollock or nipple battered as a Shrovetide football   fatty liver under a baldric
I'm often the youngest   ignored by shoppers in the high street midsummer
tickle of pheasant feather   weightless as falling conker blossom

the poor parenting decisions are waved away with a handkerchief or a smack
of hazel   centuries of steps from North Africa up through Europe
connecting our peasant culture with others   a rag on my tattyjacket for every time
I pretended not to hear our babies cry out when they wouldn't sleep

some dancers are seventy-odd   I tiptoe around their serenity   calm as a hobnail
each time their clogs click   cartilage gone in the joints   a layer of history lost

sometimes the children catch me shaking a pill bottle to the tune of Speed the Plough

I embrace the Burryman

burying my face in the crook of his neck
      to show my family I *can* be compassionate
until blood trickles from these scratched cheeks
down his back

      why would I cuddle my children for
crying at a meal they refuse to eat
when I think of all the men in my childhood?
the one who forced me to have a bath without my underpants
      something I'd done since potty training

I keep clutching to his shoulders
breathing in the burdock and whiskystink
on his balaclava
I kiss him and recoil
spitting out thistles

      the encouraged cuddle and unshaved chin
the one always late for the fortnightly visit agreed in court

though his eyes and mouth are covered
it's clear he's blubbering

      the twattish remarks about losing at snooker
constantly using the rest to play against those men

broken by ritual and wrongdoing
the bowler hat slipping
feet swollen as boiled haggis

      cigarette burns holding hands
consoling myself after a wasp sting in a paddling pool

walking ten miles in heavy boots
and August heat

I must relieve him of this greenness
offer milk to line the stomach
rub him yellow with dandelion heads
hush the penny-whistle tinnitus in his ears

The Garland King

          thumbs a cracked screen
under that dome of rhododendrons and peonies
no one has posted about his ancient custom
and now he's torment on horseback

girls in aspirin-white smocks are smirking at your daftness
they're in the moment   you're at the back of the procession
wringing out a metaphor   *you* are the one wearing blinkers
the bell-shaped bouquet hides
a hangover   each retch stifled inside the horse's canter

in your head he's had it up to the ivy with tradition
vows to wipe his arse with
Morris dancers' hankies

Jack-in-the-Green jealousy
yet you'd buckle beneath the weight of those flowers
approaching the consort
just the memory of dropping her voice
in a urinal trough
        throwing her hand-held face against the tiles

tourists cheer
a choir sings the Oak Apple Carol
red and yellow tassels cling to his shins
and your shame   he doesn't see her forced smile
bulbous sleeves or velvet gown and

under that dome of peonies and rhododendrons
        he doesn't feel the rain

Shaman

Before the first bus queue forms
he comes tumbling downhill
into the Chevin-shadowed town
like a knackered ram with a flock
of conquests in his wake.
Eyes peering out between flatcap
and thick black beard, he hears
churchbells ringing in foxgloves
falling flat on his back drunk
on Wharfe water; clears his throat
for the crows, then takes a drag
on a roll-up, unzips his overalls
to release a brace of pheasants,
bats and mice crawling past
the tobacco in his pocket –
if you look close enough you'll
see the beard covering half his face
is actually a crow, wings spread
from ear to ear.

Ellar Ghyll, he is here
to silence your bottlebanks
and fill the gully with squawk;
disrupt summer
leaning on Murphy's chimney
while some weasel slips
under bilberry like a half-yard
of ale swallowed in one.
Ellar Ghyll, hear tiny songs
and heavy breathing;
he stumbles
along rows of skips,
over nearside Vauxhall doors
in the scrapyard.
The jogger with a box
of music strapped to the bicep,
he longs to watch her squat
in steam behind a bush,
feel its dew twinkling in his whiskers.
Ellar Ghyll, console him
when she flees down Bradford Road
leaving him to weep inside
a written-off hatchback –
love rejected and crumbling
like gypsum at the tip.

III

With cupped hands
he blows three pigeon coos
through his thumbs.
Birds fill the afternoon
and watch a figure
open allotment gates,
trample rows of leeks,
to embrace a scarecrow
then pull it from the earth.
Loose hens roam the bypass
while he hobbles along
Birdcage Walk carrying
the bundle of limbs
until a dress wriggling
on a washing line
is snatched and stretched
over the scarecrow.
Should his legs give out
before reaching the Chevin,
Shaman and the straw-stuffed bride
collapse, fingers stinging
caressing nettles
that he has made her hair.

IV

Under the rustling of baking parchment where
Sunday and bread dough are brought to their knees,
he hears a radio sermon calling to those hours.
Hymn and hiccups over boiled eggs and soldiers:
a backwoods youth taught to tell time by the sun
now takes his turn as shaman of public parks;
a drake's quack and greylag's honk for the wife
who came waddling up – courting is chasing tail
where he comes from – nevermind how much hair
or teeth fall out or how grace gives way to motherhood
and a heel-toe gait punishing their floorboards.
Romance moults a little more each year
yet feathers fly when they dive in bedside light
heads hitting the pillow at the same time.

Brace

Husband and wife
laid side-by-side on the kitchen table, warm and bruised.
Palpating a breast to feel for shot –
that could be a nipple for all I know –
my son rolls up his sleeves,
five-year-old finger and thumb
pinch the hen's beak, trace
the male's collar before
I hack off each head,
grain falling from
their throats.

Solemn minutes
ripping at plumage, the room a snowglobe,
yellow skin coming away in some grasps.
The boy tells me a tail feather is a quill
while this penpusher pretends to go about
his work without guilt, remove feet and offal,
extract sinew with pliers, knowing
the hen won't lay again.
There is a change in me
now quick to bollock
the children after dinner
for something minor.

Gallows Hill

Both children run ahead,
holding our personalities like balloons,
to build insect hotels
from hogweed and string.

A wilderness has grown
out of the printing mill's spoils –
surely only weeds will sprout
from this page?

Study of a Leeds bachelor

This one needs mothering all over again
before he looks at another woman,
finding himself facedown in a litter tray
following an evening when he'd caught
his true reflection in a vomit puddle.
Cheap hotel hallways set aflame
leading someone to a room
after wooing them with a bouquet
of carnation spray once tied
to dual carriageway railings.
He would climb the highest ladder
on any pair of tights, every time
burying his nose in the gusset
of a goddess's underwear, when
all he had really done was snort up
a decoy for love. It's no more
than a toffee hammer rap on your
pubic bone when he wriggles
atop you, a fleabitten mongrel,
thinking he has covered the scent
of his competition by pissing up a shop door,
never finding solace at the end of a lapdance
and tugging at limp rope in the dark,
alone, when nights end. He awoke
staring at cat turds, wondering:
was that fidelity
or kittens picking at his bones?

Bruises beneath feathers

Heavy clouds
cast moving shadows
like a stranger walking
past your bedroom door.
Drying rain tightens skin
near Clarence Dock;
you tug the children back
from the railings,
then let down your umbrella
and use it to skewer a seagull.

You see
every hour after midnight
carrying sickly children
around Temple Newsam Farm.
No lambs or piglets
to stop the tantrums and
piece together broken sleep.
They call it straw,
you call it scarecrow guts
holding a pheasant in a headlock.

Marshalling the picnic blanket
proves too difficult amidst
quacking and the rumble of Otley pedalos.
You push the children towards
the playground, a swan waddles up
from the Wharfe, and your eyes
meet as you wring its slender neck.

There will be no one to stroke
your hand when the city's statues
are spotless and the sky is empty.
No one to hear you say sorry,
with your last breath,
for the pigeonless parks and squares,
and the canal and Aire
bereft of mallards.

Our urchin

He no longer talks: a fortnight spent in a gull-splattered
        boarding house means he only speaks
in short squeals like a common tern.

And the morning he emerged from the sea
holding a mermaid's purse, we knew he wouldn't come home
        willingly;
   he took that clutch of ray eggs in the bath with him,
awaiting the hatch of siblings – discarded in the soapdish
when they withered away.

See how dextrous he is with a chip-shop fork,
how he causes landslides of copper coins in the arcade.
He still hasn't forgiven us
        for rolling him up in a beach towel and bundling him
   onto the return coach.

To avoid further discord, we light Chinese lanterns
        every evening
so the sky above our street looks as though it is swarming
   with jellyfish.

Snap him in half and you'll find the circle of his name
   running through his core,
and somewhere off the coast his heart is trapped
        in a lobster pot.

Lawrence's voice

Crickets rub their wings together
when you clear your throat
followed by a rainbow of English
spilling from the beard.

Faint scratch of a collier's lilt
like a match being struck,
your father's coarseness:
how *without* becomes *wi'ahrt*,
round East Midlands vowels
as though you've shoved my head
in the hollow of an oak.

Those trampled mushrooms in your chest
won't even
permit a poem's recital,
wheezing then breathless
before being able to respond
to playground taunts of *mard-arse*.

Did you abandon your accent on campus,
as I did, when students from China
and Greece spoke with greater clarity?
Is that Frieda's clipped German cadence
invading the glottal stops?

I want you in all conch shells,
balsam explosion, orgasm and essay –
your whisper a post-coital pant,
an echo down a disused mineshaft.

Killing a rat with an air rifle

I remember air cadets   learning to shoot a man
with 100 for a heart   missing each time
so why can I hit you   the size of my son's cuddly toy
moving at the speed of thought

toothy librarian in the crosshairs

belly of pure white fur not as dirty as they say you are

neighbours watching
stooped low on the lawn   children in the window

the squeal and wriggle when the pellet hits
less forgettable than your lifeless tail   hard and leathery

every wire and shoelace unbearable   kettles and laptops
   connected to you
in the walls

pinching it to take you from patio to wheely bin   a pallbearer
felt every time I tie my boots

Discovery on the outskirts of Matlock

If his throat opened wide enough
to equal the Broadmoor Prison siren
then the adults who lost him would hear
a four-year-old voice moaning in the valley's basin.
Scruffy cherub wearing a halo of gnats,
a kicked pinecone led you into the ruins
of Arkwright's empire and wild garlic hell,
the thunderous Derwent drowning out
sobbing calls for help up the hill.
Approaching an old orangery with dirty windows
he pictured the lunatic, who left crazed debris
and empty bean cans scattered ahead,
sniffing out the trail of child's tears near his cave.
Give the boy a park slide and seesaw
rather than cuckoo spit and dead trees,
a lollipop to take away the taste in the air,
bitter as licking a slug's belly.
Panicstricken thrusts through weeds
disturbed Canada geese sleeping in a clearing,
honks and heavy wingbeats brought
an animal's skull into his vision.
All horror contained in that oblong head
with no skeleton lying beside it in the grass,
just a crumbling alabaster nose, hollow eyes
and the thought of being chewed in its jaws.
An amber evening drew on, as he shook
and cried in the two hours
it took his parents to find him, much older,
kindling a desire to take a toy axe to his rocking horse.

Now he fears eggs

Even if the hen dreads
a ransacking of her nest box
she'll still lay for the poultryman

who hums a tune his father once sang,
then stares through chicken wire and wonders:
"How came that lump on the boy's skull?
We are such good people... benign people."

Since seeing those little bald heads
clustered in the waiting room
he prays his hens never lay again
fingers sifting through straw, brain aching
as though it's been caved in
with a hymn book.

A man sees his own name
on a park bench plaque

for AB

Broken snowglobe glass had cut
my son's fingers that dripping-wet January
when flood waters reached the crow's nest
of the pirate-ship climbing-frame in our park –
traffic cones and scarves in the trees.
My wife's damp hair was as black as bitumen
covering the pavilion roof,
and a nursery rhyme of magpies nearby.

There might've been an argument at breakfast –
I don't recall – though I am certain,
holding the boy's bandaged hand
as he tightrope-walked along a bench,
that the raised lettering that looked at me
from the backrest, confirmed my death
some fourteen years before.

History crawled up through two counties,
out of pockets, exercise books,
and splitlipped mouths: a fight
with a would-be murderer who broke
my nose and bit me on the back –
did I die of two black eyes and tetanus?
Or was I the brother who felt
the pull of the woods one night
when he couldn't stand the town anymore?
Greens and browns flashed by
during the drop, like riding a ropeswing,
near the railway siding.

By this time, my son had grown tired
of the playground, the empty roundabout spinning.
He pointed to the woods –

I cannot refuse him the trees.

Eclipse plumage

Part the bulrushes to find
a shipwrecked dinghy where drakes once sulked,
smug bullheads twiddle their fins in the brook,
anglers drunk on pondwater
      pierce cubes of corned beef with hooks,
keep maggots warm under their tongues.

God-botched or council-built
      we thank a higher order for this water,
first blessed at the swimming baths
we gather here to be dunked in a proper baptism.

Know us by the soil beneath our fingernails
flicking V-signs to their turned backs,
arses sometimes gored by umbrella tip.
      Water pistols loaded with April showers
take aim when ducks beach, moulting and waddling
through reeds, each a dowdy brown
and flightless for a month.

      Thirty days grounded and uniform,
the males without bright feathers
all vulnerable until
midsummer when they arrow upwards again.
We leave our Bridlington-bought nets
at the midriff of the brook, upset the anglers
by throwing bread in the pond for the drakes to return
in October, restored, in full colour.

Reveille

cat's collar bell
wasps' nest in our shed rumbling
spent Catherine Wheels
still nailed to a fencepost in June
spun by wind

two talking about death
one holds up a fist
to illustrate the size of her heart
rhythmic half-clenches to make it beat
the other has an Old Testament manner
holding a washing-line prop
his accent thick as a Bible

another keeps exotic birds
in a breezeblock and wire mesh hut
tells his aviary of anecdotes

everyone is awake
all-or-nothing
cannot-wait-to-get-Xmas-over-and-done-with

creosote fumes invade the nostrils
shadows cast by cut grass
floating in a paddling pool

Three navigators, 1846

The price of wheat had risen two shillings
and the temperature had dropped in January
like the first workman to die that year; falling a hundred feet
down shaft No. 14, ascending by rope and bucket
after he had prepared a blast at the bottom
to lengthen Bramhope tunnel and open the earth.

But why should a man lower himself deep in the earth
for the reward of a purse of shillings?
His top would've been blown from his bottom
if he had not landed on the lit fuse that January
with his remains shovelled up and collected in a bucket
rather than properly buried at six feet.

Another was slain by a fragment falling seventy feet;
a teenager, not twenty years on this earth,
struck on the temple by a small stone from the bucket
perhaps the size of an acorn or a shilling.
He died like his comrade back in January
only this one was dragged up from the bottom

to take the air and recover, bottom
lip wobbling, unsteady on his feet.
A chill crept into his bones, cold as January,
after days sleeping outside on the damp earth;
the doctor covered his eyes with two shillings
a fortnight after that blunder beneath the bucket.

For the third, injustice came by the bucket-
load. Some would've left him to rot at the bottom
of the cutting and not stump up the shillings
to bury him in Pool with roses at his feet.
Crushed by falling rocks, unexpected in the earth,
too – unexpected as Christmas gifts in January.

For three days, solace remained barren as January
and still no flowers were gathered in buckets.
Finally, they found a resting place in holy earth
at Otley Parish Church, the coffin lowered to the bottom
of a grave respectfully dug, the whole 6 feet –
for some, peace takes pride over pennies and shillings.

For every person as hard and cold as earth in January,
there are tenfold who don't care for shillings; their kindness a bucket
with no bottom, steadfast to help the fallen to their feet.

A haunting at Armley Library

She led me upstairs to search the rooms for a noise;
 a tapping of keys,
skeletal fingers drumming a desk,

the slow creak of a spine bending backwards.
 I wanted to hear it
over the stifled coughs and imposed silence below,

over the century of moths and rattling blinds,
 but only her ears,
skewered by rings, caught the sound.

Dirty sash windows hung like open mouths
 as we walked the balcony
for what seemed like the lifespan of a book.

The she followed me down to meet another
 and was gone.
I looked to the shelves for my own folklore,

told myself it was coming from the clocktower –
 my veins are now ley lines
and I follow her noise each clicking hour.

Family pet used as costume for a folk play

Stretched and dried
there's scarcely half a waistcoat made from your tabby pelt
to clothe the Turkish Knight challenging St George
the beige belly tufts less than a 'kerchief's-worth
of fleece on the Derby Tup's gown
Thank you, though, for mediating during the divorce
a mouthpiece for my parents
as arguments piled up
like lumps in the litter tray

The others say I swing my wooden sword
too wildly – Beelzebub's facepaint red
as Mum's dress, her shouting in the phonebox
at the end of the street, me and the cat watching

The others say I cracked the sheep's skull
with the broomhandle playing the butcher – you were
destined for fame, the photo I took of you in front
of a lad's mag found a place above the Working Men's Club
bar, tears on the fur not visible

The others say the tortoise-shell tail
safety-pinned to my trousers is just about passable
a "fuck you" to the pigeon fancier who poisoned you
for sleeping on his shed roof

but the flea-collar bells on my boots are not allowed

A year's trigger

Texan spurs jangle
when our cutlery drawer slams shut
and I'm cowboy pulp bucked off my first quarter century.
    If this graduate's tie was a bandana
"Memory's bank raided" would headline every gazette and herald
accompanied by sepia pictures of me,
    shouldering imaginary swag,
and attempts to flatten my getaway with an anvil.

Putting down the Wild West novel,
    laying it flat on its pages like a dead bird,
there was different weather
outside each window that birthday:
        views cartooned and smothered in syrup, MIND THAT CHILD
and scrimmaging goodies and baddies
interrupted the recorder-playing
            worm charmer in the back garden soil.

        Heavy women in high heels
clip-clopping by the house were the posse
approaching, bullet belts and clutch purses,
        ready to lynch a jollygoodfellow.
After the candles, my voice broke in a goose's honk saying thank you
and the downtrodden summer sighed
    relieving our wheely bin
of plastic cups and a paper tablecloth.

A pint of maggots wriggled
    beside an angler as I walked along the towpath
with a stray greyhound and wrapping-paper-cuts.
I was expected back soon,
but I had time to remember reading in the morning and challenged
        the high noon reflection in the canal
to a duel; he was quick on the draw, loaded with foreboding,
            and empties all six barrels.

A busker leaves the brothel on York Road

circumspect as blackbirds
guitar strapped to his back;
conspicuous and giddy
he walks past the parade of shops
(shuttered frontage, newsagent, tattooist)
never had there been such music in him,
the ballad of his tingling groin,
empty bollocks knocking
together like coconuts.

The bus stop queue clutching onto
day riders and unsafe jobs
knows he has made love to everything
that's wrong with this city –
only lice and inflamed skin to show for it –
but as far as he's concerned
that was his first girlfriend
trembling on the mattress again
or the wife who left him now knocked-up;
an act that warrants whiskey
in the Irish Centre and two offerings
of 'Black Is the Colour' at
the mouth of Kirkgate Market.

Whitsuntide dray restored and paraded through Clay Cross, 2020

yellow gloss   dandelion smear when you wet the bed

shines on the beams and slats

    assembled by ghosts

Maypole ribbons   brasses depicting a cockerel and Davy Lamp

reds and blues borrowed from a Wicksteed playground

coat the wheelspokes turning after years dismantled and stored

behind cenotaph stacks of newspapers and jogging bottoms

    soiled at Infant School

hand on the bridle of a weak pony   a sugar cube before each hill

rubbing her piebald muzzle on High Street, empty

    except for a Kinder Egg capsule trodden

    into a dog turd

collapsed trampolines in backyards   parked toy motorbikes in gardens

the dray clatters past the commemorative coal tub and rockery
housewives leave piles of ironing   tears speckling the yoke of a shirt
to stand on doorsteps stoic as greyhounds
a father praised for smacking the children only once
        alights the toilet without wiping to watch
other husbands who drink cans of bitter with a foxhunter on the label
        and complain about class

then children arrive   like photos developed at the chemists
        and join the procession   skipping and capering
somehow the pony grows and has Shire-like quarters and plaited fetlocks
the rumble shakes dust from shirting boards like newlyweds in bed
coppers jangling in a family of Natwest piggybanks

we reach the cricket pavilion at the Miners' Welfare
flies wriggling on the tables of biscuits and cake
the May Queen spits a dead wasp drowned in her flat pop
you look at the crowds in the sun   the colours, the violent joy
like a fresh tattoo of a swallow on a forearm

witch

she has made an altar
on our porch windowsill
forsythia branches crane over
quartz stones arranged in circles
to protect the children

I'm no longer startled
by the healing oils on the pantry shelves
next to mustard and curry paste jars
or by the stickiness of calendula stamens
when we kiss

palming her hair she complains
about grey poisoning the brown
but I'm drawn to turkeytails
fanning out around her neck

heart-shaped ivy spills
from a plantpot in the kitchen
and I wonder what charm is this
making me giddily sweep up earth
fallen from beneath her toenails
and search teapot dregs
emptied in the sink
hoping for some mention of me
in the leaves?

Poem that features lines from
a song heard in Stoney Middleton

There were three ravens in a tree
        seen from a distance of centuries
before stones enclosed these fields
          muscling out the foxgloves
The middlemost raven said to me,
"There lies a dead man at yon tree"
      beak thick as Dad's liver
         history eclipsed by the hills

There comes his lady full of woe
      frail as those that die of drink
helping her over a stile   painted eyes
        under the veil
There comes his lady full of woe
bending her head *as she could go*
      to inspect the crumpled overalls
         feathers laid around in an oval

"Who's this that's killed my own true love,"
      she said in my mother's voice
and untied a lace on her dress dropping
        straw in the grass
"I hope in heaven he'll never rest
Nor e'er enjoy that blessed place."
        nothing left but straw and rags and a fear
         that keeps birds in the oak

Notes on the Text

16. Well Dressing is the decoration of wells with flowers at Whitsuntide, especially in Derbyshire, as an ancient custom originally associated with the belief in water deities. (Oxford English Dictionary)

20. A mummers' play consists of a simple plot in which two participants fight until one is killed. A doctor then appears and brings the dead man back to life. It seems that mummers often performed their plays primarily as a means of making money, and this is certainly the case in North-East Derbyshire.

23. Contains lyrics from a song traditionally performed on Flora Day, May 1st, in Helston, Cornwall

25. In the North of England, as early as the 1800s, a procession would gather at dusk armed with "culinary weapons", banging pots and pans, playing tin whistles, making a general racket, carrying a youth on a length of wood (stang). This was to recognise a "matrimonial difference" and make an example of a man who beat his wife. The procession ended at the door of the unhappy household where the youth would recite a song or poem (extracts taken from 'Punishments in the Olden Time' by William Andrews).

28. Balter: To dance clumsily; to tumble.

30. The Burryman – On the second Friday of August a man is dressed from head to ankle in approximately 11,000 burrs and paraded through the South Queensferry area of Edinburgh. The custom was first recorded in 1687 but it is believed to be older, and one folklorist describes the tradition as "an ordeal".

32.   The Garland King – Each year on May 29th, a man is dressed, head to waist, in flowers then leads a procession through the town of Castleton, Derbyshire with a woman wearing Tudor costume. The custom is believed to have started in 1660 to commemorate the restoration of Charles II, but some folklorists believe it to be much older.

33.   The Chevin is a 900ft-high ridge that overlooks the market town of Otley, West Yorkshire.

38.   Gallows Hill is a nature reserve in Otley, West Yorkshire – the last person to be hanged there was the Town Crier in 1614

46.   The song Edward (the namesake of the author's second child) features in *Eighty English folk songs from the Southern Appalachians* by Cecil Sharp and Maud Karpeles and begins with the question: "How came the blood on your shirtsleeve?"

61.   "I am favoured with the copy here presented by Mr John Holmes, of Roundhay, who first heard it about 1825 from his mother's singing. This was in a remote village among the Derbyshire hills, most aptly named Stoney Middleton," *Traditional Tunes* by Frank Kidson.

Acknowledgements

Poems from this collection first appeared in *butcher's dog*, Greenteeth Press's *Unhomely* anthology, *Hinterland*, *The Leeds Debacle*, *Magma*, *The Morning Star*, *Project 154 – Live Canon*, *Shearsman*, *Strix*, *The Valley Press Anthology of Yorkshire Poetry* and Yaffle Press's *And the Stones Fell Open* anthology.

The 'Shaman' sequence and 'Three Navigators, 1846' were commissioned by Otley Town Council as part of the Town Poet scheme, and published in *Otley Matters*.

'Most of the cargo was dead before the accident', 'Collecting post from a previous address' and 'A year's trigger' were published by Ossett Observer as part of their Arts Council-funded project *A Firm of Poets: Holding Your Hand Through Hard Times*.

Thank you to Peter Spafford and Thomas Kade for commissioning 'Reveille' for LeedsDortmund50.

Thank you to Dr Helen Mort and William Thirsk-Gaskill for including 'A busker leaves the brothel on York Road' in Dr Mort's Leads to Leeds project.

Thank you to Adult Teeth Recording Company for releasing recordings of some of these poems on the 'Runt County' album. And thank you to BBC 6 Music for playing them.

'Discovery on the Outskirts of Matlock' was commissioned by Leeds Lieder Day of Song.

***

Unfathomable thanks to Becky Cherriman who has supported me during the writing of this book. Thank you to Otley Poets and Otley Poetry Gym for feedback on some of these poems, and to Glenis Burgess, Sandra Burnett and Jane Kite who have been so encouraging throughout my time as Otley Town Poet, and I am grateful to Otley Town Council for continuing to fund the Town Poet Scheme. Thank you to Ben Edge for his inspirational paintings and for the use of 'The Garland King', and to Leeds Libraries for keeping such fantastic texts on folk customs, dancing and song. And a jolly wassail to Wharfedale Wayzgoose Border Morris for the dancing, singing and wonderful times.

Thank you to Jamie McGarry at Valley Press for his friendship and encouragement, to Martha Sprackland for her editorial skills, and to Peter Barnfather for his marvellous page design.

I am always grateful to my teachers at Tupton Hall School who introduced me to poetry, Pete Bunten, Rob Hudson and Nigel Whitaker, to Harriet Tarlo, my poetry tutor at Bretton Hall, and to Jimmy Andrex, John Irving Clarke and Gareth Durasow for seeing me through to poetic adulthood.

Lastly, thank you to my beautiful family and friends.